This book belongs to:

Heckerty's Christmas
Story: Ann Rachlin, Jan Ziff and Allan Davidson
Illustrations: Francesca da Sacco and Sparganum

Copy Editors: Jan Ziff and Allan Davidson
Design and Layout: Sparganum, Allan Davidson and Jan Ziff

Created from an original idea by Ann and Ezra Rachlin

ISBN 978-1-63150-011-4

Contact us at:

 www.heckerty.com   @LoveHeckerty

 heckerty@heckerty.com   LoveHeckerty

For Ezra, Ann and Iain – Heckerty's "parents". And all of Heckerty and Zanzibar's many friends, who believed in them and helped bring them to life.

Our deepest appreciation to all of you who encouraged, backed, advised and supported Heckerty, without expecting or wanting public acknowledgement.

Had it not been for you, Heckerty wouldn't be here today!

Apps, Books, eBooks & Audio Books

COLLECT THEM ALL!

 Free Download

www.heckerty.com

HECKERTY'S CHRISTMAS

By Ann Rachlin, Jan Ziff and Allan Davidson

Illustrations by Francesca da Sacco and Sparganum

I was just sitting down to breakfast with Zanzibar, my cat, when my front door opened all by itself.

There stood my perfectly turned-out
cousin, Persnickerty.
Cloak swirling, she sailed into my
cave, sweeping Zanzibar
out of her way.

"Come along, Heckerty," she ordered. "It's time for your Christmas present. I've come up with a fabulous plan which I know you'll love."

I looked at Zanzibar, who looked at me. We both stared at her.

What could she mean?

"It's makeover time," announced Persnickerty with a flourish.

"I've booked you into the Spellbound Beauty Parlor.

And we're going there now!"

There was a flash, a swoosh,
and hundreds of sparkly stars
in red and green.

When I opened my eyes, I was
sitting in a chair with a stylist
hovering nearby.

"Tidy her up," commanded Persnickerty.

"Her hair looks like a rat's nest. Make it smooth and shiny, just like mine."

Next, she turned to a small, bald man with a long measuring tape round his neck.

"Look at her terrible, tattered clothes," she said.

"Heckerty needs a new cloak, one that swishes and swirls, just like mine."

"And now her hat," continued Persnickerty. "Her battered and patched hat with its broken brim.

"Take it away! And make her a beautiful witch's hat, just like mine."

"Now Heckerty," she said. "Sit still and stop wriggling!" Then she snapped her fingers, and her broomstick instantly flew over.

"Ah, yes," said Persnickerty, "I almost forgot your broomstick.

"It's not even good enough for firewood.

"I've ordered a new one, just like mine.

"I'll be back!"

And in a shower of pink hearts
and silver sparkles, she was gone.

Everyone
got to work.

My hair was
washed
and pulled.

And pulled,
and pulled.

The little man ran around me measuring and waving his hands. His assistant started cutting and sewing. I closed my eyes. I didn't want any part of this but couldn't see how to stop it.

Suddenly Persnickerty
was back.

"Stand up!"
She ordered me.

"Now look at yourself in the mirror."

I opened my eyes and stared
and stared and stared.

It was
the same me.
With **my green
face** it couldn't be
anyone else.

But that was the
only thing
about me that I
did recognize.

The small, bald man presented me with a beautiful new cloak. I put it on over my patched orange coat and it swished and swirled, just like Persnickerty's.

The hat was beautiful. Marvelous.

And it was pointed and shiny,
just like Persnickerty's.

Then
I looked in
the mirror.

The neat
and tidy
person
with the
green face
staring back
at me didn't
look like me
at all.

Persnickerty was very pleased with herself. "Happy Christmas, Heckerty,"

she said. "You look wonderful.
Try to keep yourself this way."

"And to complete your makeover, here is the latest in broomsticks.

"It's fast and it doesn't fly upside down, it's just like mine."

I thanked her for my Christmas presents, climbed on the new broomstick and headed home.

I opened the door
of the cave
and went in.

Zanzibar came slowly towards the door.

His eyes got bigger and bigger.

"Who are you?" he hissed.

"It's me, Zanz," I said.
"It's me, Heckerty.

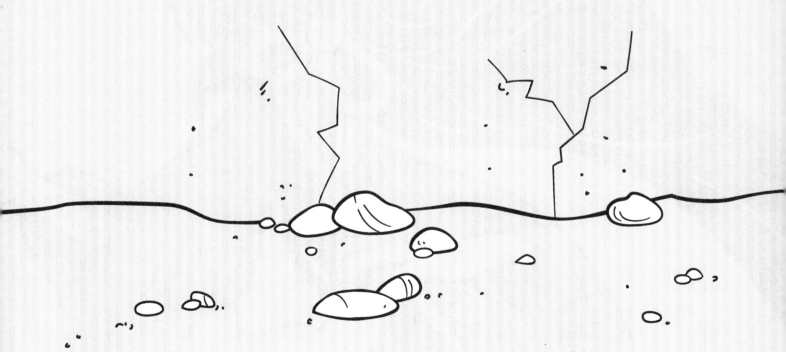

"Don't you know me any more?"

"GO AWAY!"

"You are NOT my Heckerty!
You aren't! You aren't!"

he yelled.

And he shrieked and howled and ran
into the back of the cave.

He was gone.

I was so unhappy, I had to go out.
Maybe flying around would help.

I was high above a field
when I heard someone crying.

I flew down to see who it was.

It was a little old witch with white hair, and she was shivering.

"What's wrong?" I asked her.

"I'm so cold," she said. "There was a big storm, and I was thrown all over the sky. When it was over, my cloak was gone.

"I'm freezing," she moaned.
Her teeth chattered.

"There!"

I said.
"You need this more
than I do. Happy
Christmas!"

She looked at
me wide-eyed.
"Thank you,"
she said.
"Thank you very
much."

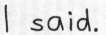

I climbed back on
the broom and
flew off towards
the river.

Down below me I saw a bald wizard,
climbing up in a tree, looking very upset.

Once again,
I flew down
to see what
was wrong. His hat had
caught on the top of a thorn bush and
had been ripped to shreds.

I took off my new shiny hat and
gave it to him. "There!" I said.
"You need this more than I do.
Happy Christmas!"

He looked at me in amazement.

"Thank you," he said.
"Thank you very much."

I turned the broomstick
to go home.

The wind whistled around my head,
and my straight hair began to curl.

Soon it looked like it always did,
curly and frizzy.

I was close to my cave
when I saw a small family
standing in the road.

Christmas presents were
all around them.

For the third time,
I flew down to see what
was wrong.

"Our broomstick
broke," they
said sadly. "We had so
many presents to give to
people for Christmas.

"We must have overloaded it,
and it snapped into three pieces.

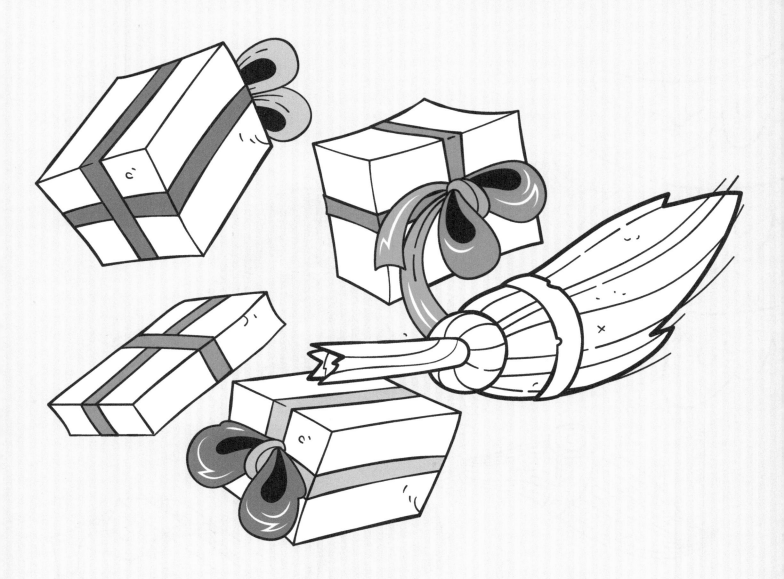

"Now we can't have Christmas with our family, and the children won't have their presents."

"Don't be upset," I told them.
"I can fix it."

"How?" They asked – holding out three broken pieces of wood.

I gave them my new broomstick, the fast one, the one that didn't fly upside down.

"You need it more than I do,"
I said. "Happy Christmas."

As I walked away, I could hear them laughing merrily as they loaded the presents onto the broomstick.

Happy again, they flew away into the night.

I trudged home. I was **so tired.**
And I was worried what Zanzibar would
say when he saw me.

As I got close to the cave,
there was Zanzibar waiting for me.

"Heckerty!"
He squealed, hugging me and
dancing round and round.

"It IS you –
and you look just like yourself again!"

I looked at myself in the mirror and smiled and smiled. My hair was frizzy. My old coat was torn and patched.

"Happy Christmas, Heckerty,"
said Zanzibar.

"This is the best present of all. I
have my Heckerty back! Just the
way she always is, kind and loving."

Even my broomstick agreed, rustling its twigs to show how pleased it was that I was back at home.

"Happy Christmas, Zanz," I said.
"Let's hang up our stockings and wait
for Father Christmas."

And we did.

Love from Heckerty

Lightning Source UK Ltd.
Milton Keynes UK
UKOW07f0640071015

260018UK00007B/55/P

9 781631 500114